Faith Healer

Brian Friel was born in Omagh, County Tyrone, in 1929. His plays include *Philadelphia, Here I Come!*, *Translations*, *Faith Healer*, *Making History*, *Dancing at Lughnasa*, *The Home Place* and *Performances*.

'Brian Friel is one of the most accomplished playwrights working in English today. His work is developed around a central poetic vision, which has found, and enhanced, a language of the theatre to communicate difficult ideas. This language of drama works through wider poetic sensibilities we actually share with the playwright but which we have lost sight of. Brian Friel sharpens our perceptions and makes us able to understand our human condition and the deepening ironies and contradictions of our age. This is his poetic vision.' Michael Etherton, *Contemporary Irish Dramatists* (Macmillan)

by the same author

also available

BRIAN FRIEL

Faith Healer

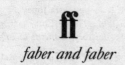

faber and faber

First published in this edition 2001
by Faber and Faber Limited
3 Queen Square, London WC1N 3AU

Typeset by Country Setting, Kingsdown, Kent CT14 8ES
Printed in England by Mackays of Chatham plc, Chatham, Kent

A CIP record for this book
is available from the British Library

ISBN 978-0-571-21458-7
ISBN 0-571-21458-4

2 4 6 8 10 9 7 5 3

Faith Healer was first produced at the Longacre
Theatre, New York, on 5 April 1979. The cast was
as follows:

Frank James Mason
Grace Clarissa Kaye
Teddy Donal Donnelly

Direction José Quintero

Note

Stage directions have been kept to a minimum.
In all four parts the director will decide when and
where the monologist sits, walks, stands, etc.

For Anne again

Part One

FRANK

The stage is in darkness. Brief pause.

*Then out of this darkness comes Frank's
incantation, 'Aberarder, Aberayron . . .' At the end
of the second line bring up lights very slowly, first
around him and then gradually on the whole set.
Throughout this opening incantation he is standing
downstage left, feet together, his face tilted upwards,
his eyes shut tight, his hands in his overcoat pockets,
his shoulders hunched.*

*He is middle-aged; grey or greying; pale, lined face.
The overcoat is unbuttoned, the collar up at the back;
either navy or black, and of heavy-nap material; a
good coat once but now shabby, stained, slept-in.
Underneath he is wearing a dark suit that is polished
with use; narrow across the shoulders; sleeves and legs
too short. A soiled white shirt. A creased tie. Vivid
green socks.*

*Three rows of chairs – not more than fifteen seats
in all – occupy one-third of the acting area stage left.
These seats are at right angles to the audience.*

On the backdrop is a large poster:

THE FANTASTIC FRANCIS HARDY

FAITH HEALER

ONE NIGHT ONLY

*This poster is made of some fabric, linen perhaps, and
is soiled and abused.*

Frank (*eyes closed*)
   Aberarder, Aberayron,
   Llangranog, Llangurig,
   Abergorlech, Abergynolwyn,
   Llandefeilog, Llanerchymedd,
   Aberhosan, Aberporth . . .
All those dying Welsh villages. (*Eyes open.*) I'd get so
tense before a performance, d'you know what I used
to do? As we drove along those narrow, winding roads
I'd recite the names to myself just for the mesmerism,
the sedation, of the incantation –
   Kinlochbervie, Inverbervie,
   Inverdruie, Invergordon,
   Badachroo, Kinlochewe,
   Ballantrae, Inverkeithing,
   Cawdor, Kirkconnel,
   Plaidy, Kirkinner . . .
Welsh – Scottish – over the years they became
indistinguishable. The kirks or meeting-houses or
schools – all identical, all derelict. Maybe in a corner
a withered sheaf of wheat from a harvest thanksgiving
of years ago or a fragment of a Christmas decoration
across a window – relicts of abandoned rituals.
Because the people we moved among were beyond
that kind of celebration.
   Hardly ever cities or towns because the halls were
far too dear for us. Seldom England because Teddy
and Gracie were English and they believed, God help
them, that the Celtic temperament was more receptive
to us. And never Ireland because of me –
   I beg your pardon – The *Fantastic Francis Hardy,
Faith Healer, One Night Only*. (*A slight bow.*) The
man on the tatty banner.

2

He takes off his overcoat, selects an end chair from one of the rows, and throws the coat across it. This chair and coat will be in the same position at the opening of Part Four.

When we started out – oh, years and years ago – we used to have *Francis Hardy, Seventh Son of a Seventh Son* across the top. But it made the poster too expensive and Teddy persuaded me to settle for the modest 'fantastic'. It was a favourite word of his and maybe in this case he employed it with accuracy. As for the Seventh Son – that was a lie. I was in fact the only child of elderly parents, Jack and Mary Hardy, born in the village of Kilmeedy in County Limerick where my father was sergeant of the guards. But that's another story . . .

The initials were convenient, weren't they? FH – Faith Healer. Or if you were a believer in fate, you might say my life was determined the day I was christened. Perhaps if my name had been Charles Potter I would have been . . . Cardinal Primate; or Patsy Muldoon, the Fantastic Prime Minister. No, I don't mock those things. By no means. I'm not respectful but I don't mock.

Faith healer – faith healing. A craft without an apprenticeship, a ministry without responsibility, a vocation without a ministry. How did I get involved? As a young man I chanced to flirt with it and it possessed me. No, no, no, no, no – that's rhetoric. No; let's say I did it . . . because I could do it. That's accurate enough. And occasionally it worked – oh, yes, occasionally it *did* work. Oh, yes. And when it did, when I stood before a man and placed my hands on him and watched him become whole in my presence,

those were nights of exultation, of consummation –
no, not that I was doing good, giving relief, spreading
joy – good God, no, nothing at all to do with that;
but because the questions that undermined my life
then became meaningless and because I knew that for
those few hours I had become whole in myself, and
perfect in myself, and in a manner of speaking, an
aristocrat, if the term doesn't offend you.

But the questionings, the questionings . . . They
began modestly enough with the pompous struttings
of a young man: *Am I endowed with a unique and
awesome gift?* – my God, yes, I'm afraid so. And
I suppose the other extreme was *Am I a con man?* –
which of course was nonsense, I think. And between
those absurd exaggerations the possibilities were
legion. Was it all chance? – or skill? – or illusion? –
or delusion? Precisely what power did I possess?
Could I summon it? When and how? Was I its servant?
Did it reside in my ability to invest someone with faith
in me or did I evoke from him a healing faith in
himself? Could my healing be effected without faith?
But faith in what? – in me? – in the possibility? –
faith in faith? And is the power diminishing? You're
beginning to masquerade, aren't you? You're becoming
a husk, aren't you? And so it went on and on and on.
Silly, wasn't it? Considering that nine times out of ten
nothing at all happened. But they persisted right to the
end, those nagging, tormenting, maddening questions
that rotted my life. When I refused to confront them,
they ambushed me. And when they threatened to
submerge me, I silenced them with whiskey. That was
efficient for a while. It got me through the job night
after night. And when nothing happened or when
something did happen, it helped me to accept that.

But I can tell you this: there was one thing I did know, one thing I always knew right from the beginning – I always knew, drunk or sober, I always knew when nothing was going to happen.

Teddy. Yes, let me tell you about Teddy, my manager. Cockney. Buoyant. Cheerful. Tiny nimble feet. Dressed in cord jacket, bow-tie, greasy velour hat. I never knew much about his background except that he had been born into show business. And I never understood why he stayed with me because we barely scraped a living. But he had a devotion to me and I think he had a vague sense of being associated with something . . . spiritual and that gave him satisfaction. If you met him in a bar he'd hold you with those brown eyes of his. 'I've 'andled some of *the* most sensational properties in my day, dear 'eart, believe me. But I've threw 'em all up for Mr 'ardy 'ere, 'cos 'e is just the most fantastic fing you've ever seen.' And listening to him I'd almost forget what indeed he had given up to tour with us – a Miss Mulatto and Her Three Pigeons, and a languid whippet called Rob Roy who took sounds from a set of bagpipes. Humbling precedents, if I were given to pride. And he believed all along and right up to the end that somewhere one day something 'fantastic' was going to happen to us. 'Believe me, dear 'eart,' perhaps when we had barely enough petrol to take us to the next village, 'believe me, we are on the point of making a killing.' He was a romantic man. And when he talked about this killing, I had a fairy-tale image of us being summoned to some royal bedroom and learned doctors being pushed aside and I'd raise the sleeping princess to life and we'd be wined and dined for seven days and seven nights and sent on our way with bags of sovereigns. But he was a man of many disguises. Perhaps he wasn't romantic. Perhaps he knew that's what I'd think. Perhaps he was a much more perceptive man than I knew.

And there was Grace, my mistress. A Yorkshire woman. Controlled, correct, methodical, orderly. Who fed me, washed and ironed for me, nursed me, humoured me. Saved me, I'm sure, from drinking myself to death. Would have attempted to reform me because that was her nature, but didn't because her instincts were wiser than her impulses. Grace Dodsmith from Scarborough – or was it Knaresborough? I don't remember, they all sound so alike it doesn't matter. She never asked for marriage and for all her tidiness I don't think she wanted marriage – her loyalty was adequate for her. And it was never a heady relationship, not even in the early days. But it lasted. A surviving relationship. And yet as we grew older together I thought it wouldn't. Because that very virtue of hers – that mulish, unquestioning, indefatigable loyalty – settled on us like a heavy dust. And nothing I did, neither my bitterness nor my deliberate neglect nor my blatant unfaithfulness, could disturb it.

We'd arrive in the van usually in the early evening. Pin up the poster. Arrange the chairs and benches. Place a table inside the door for the collection. Maybe sweep the place out. Gracie'd make tea on the primus stove. Teddy'd try out his amplifying system. I'd fortify myself with some drink. Then we'd wait. And wait. And as soon as darkness fell, a few would begin to sidle in –

Penllech, Pencader,
Dunvegan, Dunblane,

6

Ben Lawers, Ben Rinnes,
Kirkliston, Bennane . . .

Teddy and his amplifying system: I fought with him
about it dozens of times and finally gave in to him.
Our row was over what he called 'atmospheric
background music'. When the people would have
gathered Teddy would ask them – he held the
microphone up to his lips and assumed a special,
reverential tone – he'd ask them to stay in their seats
while I moved among them. 'Everybody'll be attended
to, dear 'eart. Relax. Take it easy. And when Mr 'ardy
gets to you, no need to tell 'im wot's bovvering you –
Mr 'ardy knows. Just trust 'im. Put yourself in 'is
'ands. And God bless you all. And now, dear 'eart –
Mr 'ardy, Faif 'ealer!' At which point I'd emerge – and
at the same moment Teddy'd put on his record.

And as I'd move from seat to seat, among the
crippled and the blind and the disfigured and the deaf
and the barren, a voice in the style of the thirties
crooned Jerome Kern's song:

Lovely, never, never change,
Keep that breathless charm,
Won't you please arrange it,
'Cause I love you
Just the way you look tonight.

Yes; we were always balanced somewhere between the
absurd and the momentous.

(*Moving through seats*) And the people who came –
what is there to say about them? They were a despairing
people. That they came to me, a mountebank, was a
measure of their despair. They seldom spoke. Sometimes
didn't even raise their eyes. They just sat there, very
still, assuming that I divined their complaints. Abject.
Abased. Tight. Longing to open themselves and at the

same time fearfully herding the anguish they contained against disturbance. And they hated me – oh, yes, yes, yes, they hated me. Because by coming to me they exposed, publicly acknowledged, their desperation. And even though they told themselves they were here because of the remote possibility of a cure, they knew in their hearts they had come not to be cured but for confirmation that they were incurable; not in hope but for the elimination of hope; for the removal of that final, impossible chance – that's why they came – to seal their anguish, for the content of a finality.

And they knew that I knew. And so they defied me to endow them with hopelessness. But I couldn't do even that for them. And they knew I couldn't. A peculiar situation, wasn't it? No, not peculiar – eerie. Because occasionally, just occasionally, the miracle would happen. And then – panic – panic – panic! Their ripping apart! The explosion of their careful calculations! The sudden flooding of dreadful, hopeless hope! I often thought it would have been a kindness to them not to go near them.

And there was another thing about them. When Teddy was introducing me, I would look at them and sometimes I got a strange sense that they weren't there on their own behalf at all but as delegates, *legati*, chosen because of their audacity; and that outside, poised, mute, waiting in the half-light, were hundreds of people who held their breath while we were in the locality. And I sometimes got the impression, too, that if we hadn't come to them, they would have sought us out.

We were in the north of Scotland when I got word that my mother had had a heart attack. In a village called Kinlochbervie, in Sutherland, about as far north as you can go in Scotland. A picturesque little place, very quiet, very beautiful, looking across to the Isle of Lewis in the Outer Hebrides; and we were enjoying a few days rest there. Anyhow, when the news came, Teddy drove me down to Glasgow. Gracie wanted to come with me and couldn't understand when I wouldn't take her. But she used her incomprehension as fuel for her loyalty and sent me off with a patient smile.

It was my first time home in twenty years. My father had retired and was living in a housing estate outside Dublin. When he opened the door he didn't recognize me – I had to tell him who I was. Then he shook my hand as if I were an acquaintance and led me up to the bedroom.

She was exactly as I remembered her – illness hadn't ravaged her. Sleeping silently. Her skin smooth and girlish, her chin raised as if in expectation. Jesus, I thought, O my Jesus, what am I going to do?

'She looks nice,' he said.

'Yes,' I said. 'She looks great.'

He cleared his throat.

'She passed away quietly. You missed her by approximately one hour and ten minutes,' as if he were giving evidence. And then he cried.

And I felt such overwhelming relief that when he cried, I cried easily with him.

Twelve years later I was back in Ireland again; with Teddy and Gracie. Things had been lean for a long time. Or as Teddy put it, 'If we want to eat, we've got to open up new territory, dear 'eart. You've cured 'em all 'ere. Come on – let's go to the lush pickings of Ireland.' And I agreed because I was as heartsick of Wales and Scotland as they were. And the whiskey wasn't as efficient with the questions as it had been.

And my father had died in the meantime. And I suppose because I always knew we would end up there. So on the last day of August we crossed from Stranraer to Larne and drove through the night to County Donegal. And there we got lodgings in a pub, a lounge bar, really, outside a village called Ballybeg, not far from Donegal Town.

There was no sense of home-coming. I tried to simulate it but nothing stirred. Only a few memories, wan and neutral. One of my father watching me through the bars of the dayroom window as I left for school – we lived in a rented house across the street. One of playing with handcuffs, slipping my hands in and out through the rings. One of my mother making bread and singing a hymn to herself. 'Yes, heaven, yes, heaven, yes, heaven is the prize.' And one of a group of men being shown over the barracks – I think they were inspectors from Dublin – and my father saying, 'Certainly, gentlemen, by all means, gentlemen, anything you say, gentlemen.' Maybe one or two other memories. They evoked nothing.

When we came downstairs to the lounge in the pub we got caught up in the remnants of a wedding party – four young men, locals, small farmers, whose friend had just gone off on his honeymoon a few hours earlier. Good suits. White carnations. Dark, angular faces. Thick fingers and black nails. For a while they pretended to ignore us. Then Ned, the biggest of them, asked bluntly who we were and what we were. Teddy told them. 'Dear 'eart . . . the . . . most . . . sensational . . . fantastic.' And either at the extravagance of the introduction or because of an unease they suddenly exploded with laughter and we were embraced. We formed a big circle and drank and

chatted. Gracie sang – 'Ilkley Moor'? – something like
that. Teddy entertained them with tales of our tours
ranging from the outrageous to the maudlin and ended
with his brown eyes moist with tears: 'Dear 'earts, the
insights it 'as given me into tortured 'umanity.' And
I told myself that I was indeed experiencing a
home-coming. All irony was suspended.

Then suddenly a man called Donal who had scarcely
spoken up to this thrust a bent finger in front of my
face and challenged, 'Straighten that, Mr Hardy.' And
the bar went still.

I caught the finger between the palms of my hands
and held it there and looked into his face. Already he
was uneasy – he wanted to withdraw the challenge.
He began to stammer how the accident happened –
something about a tractor, a gearbox, a faulty setting.
And as he spoke I massaged the finger. And when he
stopped talking I opened my hands and released him.
The finger was whole . . .

Badrallach, Kilmore,
Llanfaethlu, Llanfechell,
Kincardine, Kinross,
Loughcarron, Lougligelly . . .

We caroused right through the night. Toasts to the
landlord who claimed he met my father once and as
the night went on that they were close friends. Toasts
to Teddy and Gracie. Toasts to my return. To Donal's
finger. Toasts to the departed groom and his prowess.
To the bride and her fertility. To the rich harvest – the
corn, the wheat, the barley. Toasts to all Septembers
and all harvests and to all things ripe and eager for
the reaper. A Dionysian night. A Bacchanalian night.
A frenzied, excessive Irish night when ritual was
consciously and relentlessly debauched.

Then sometime before dawn McGarvey was remembered. Their greatest, their closest friend McGarvey who in his time had danced with them and drunk with them and built roads with them and cut turf with them. McGarvey who ought to have been best man that day – my God, who else? – and who wasn't even at the wedding reception. And as they created him I saw McGarvey in my mind, saw his strained face and his mauve hands and his burning eyes, crouched in his wheelchair and sick with bitterness. Saw him and knew him before Teddy in his English innocence asked why he wasn't there; before Ned told us of the fall from the scaffolding and the paralysis. Saw him and recognized our meeting: an open place, a walled yard, trees, orange skies, warm wind. And knew, knew with cold certainty that nothing was going to happen. Nothing at all.

I stood at the window and watched them set off to fetch McGarvey. Four of them getting into a battered car; now serious and busy with good deeds; now being polite to one another, holding doors open, you sit in front, no you, no you. Then they were gone, the car sluggish under their weight.

Teddy lay slumped in a stupor in a corner. Gracie went round the tables, emptying ashtrays, gathering glasses and leaving them on the counter, straightening chairs. No intimation whatever of danger. I suggested she should go to bed and she went off. Why wouldn't she? – the housework was finished.

He comes right down, walking very slowly, until he is as close as he can be to the audience. Pause.

The first Irish tour! The great home-coming! The new beginning! It was all going to be so fantastic! And

there I am, pretending to subscribe to the charade.
(*He laughs.*) Yes; the restoration of Francis Hardy.
(*Laughs again.*)

But we'll come to that presently. Or as Teddy
would have put it: Why don't we leave that until later,
dear 'eart? Why don't we do that? Why not?

Indeed.

He looks at the audience for about three seconds.
Then quick black.

Part Two

GRACE

*We discover Grace Hardy on stage, the same set as
Part One, with the rows of seats removed. She is
sitting on a wooden chair beside a small table on
which are ashtrays, packets of cigarettes, the remains
of a bottle of whiskey, a glass.*

*She is in early middle age. Indifferent to her
appearance and barely concealing her distraught
mental state. Smoking a lot – sometimes lighting one
cigarette from the other.*

Grace (*eyes closed*)
Aberarder, Aberayron,
Llangranog, Llangurig,
Abergorlech, Abergynolwyn,
Penllech, Pencader,
Llandefeilog, Llanerchymedd . . .
That most persistent of all the memories, (*Eyes open.*)
that most persistent and most agonizing –
But I *am* getting stronger, I *am* becoming more
controlled – I'm sure I am. I measure my progress – a
silly index, I know, and he would certainly have scoffed
at it – but I can almost measure my progress by the
number of hours I sleep and the amount I drink and
the number of cigarettes I smoke. And, as they say,
I've a lot to be thankful for; I know I have. And I like
living in London. And the bedsitter's small but it's
warm and comfortable. And it's a pleasant walk to
the library in Paddington where I work four hours

every morning. And on my way home, if the day's
fine, I usually go through the park. And at night I
listen to the radio or I read – oh, I read a lot – fiction,
romance, history, biography, whatever I take home
with me, whatever's handy; and I've begun to make a
rug for the hearth – I'll do a bit at that or maybe I'll
try a new recipe or read the paper or knit or – or –
And on Thursday afternoons I go to the doctor to get
my pills renewed. He said to me last week, he said to
me, 'Of course you've had a traumatic experience,
Mrs Hardy; absolutely horrific. But it's over – finished
with. And you've really got to be stern with yourself.
You were a solicitor once, weren't you? Well, what
you must do now is bring the same mental rigour, the
same discipline to your recovery that you once brought
to a legal case.' And he looked so pleased with his
analogy and so clean and so pleasant and so efficient
and, yes, so innocent, sitting there behind his desk
with his grey suit and his college tie and his clear eyes
and his gold pen poised, and he meant so well and he
was so patient and it was all so simple for him; and
I found myself nodding yes, yes, yes to him, yes, yes;
and I thought: That's how you used to nod to Frank,
too, especially in that last year – yes, yes, yes, Frank,
you know you can, Frank, I swear you can – but he's
watching me warily – nothing was simple for him –
he's watching me and testing me with his sly questions
and making his own devious deductions, probing my
affirmations for the hair-crack, tuned for the least hint
of excess or uncertainty, but all the same, all the same
drawing sustenance from me – oh, yes, I'm sure of
that – finding some kind of sustenance in me – I'm
absolutely sure of that, because finally he drained me,
finally I was exhausted.

But I *am* making progress. And I suppose what I really mean by that is that there are certain restricted memories that I can invite now, that I can open myself fully to, like a patient going back to solids. I can think about the night the old farmer outside Cardiff gave him £200 for curing his limp – just handed him his wallet – and we booked into the Royal Abercorn and for four nights we lived like kings. And the weekend we spent one Easter walking in the Grampian mountains. I can think about that; yes, memories like that I can receive and respond to them. Because they *were* part of our lives together. But then as soon as I begin to open under them, just as soon as it seems that I'm beginning to come together again –

(*Eyes closed tight.*)

Abergorlech, Abergynolwyn,
Llandefeilog, Llanerchymedd,
Aberhosan, Aberporth . . .

It's winter, it's night, it's raining, the Welsh roads are narrow, we're on our way to a performance. (*Eyes open.*) He always called it a performance, teasing the word with that mocking voice of his – 'Where do I perform tonight?' 'Do you expect a performance in a place like this?' – as if it were a game he might take part in only if he felt like it, maybe because that was the only way he could talk about it. Anyhow Teddy's driving as usual, and I'm in the passenger seat, and he's immediately behind us, the Fantastic Francis Hardy, Faith Healer, with his back to us and the whiskey bottle between his legs, and he's squatting on the floor of the van – no, not squatting – crouched, wound up, concentrated, and happy – no, not happy, certainly not happy, I don't think he ever knew what happiness was – but always before a performance he'd be . . . in complete mastery – yes, that's close to it – in such complete mastery that everything is harmonised for him, in such mastery that anything is possible. And when you speak to him he turns his head and looks beyond you with those damn benign eyes of his, looking past you out of his completion, out of that private power, out of that certainty that was accessible only to him. God, how I resented that privacy! And he's reciting the names of all those dying Welsh villages – Aberarder, Aberayron, Llangranog, Llangurig – releasing them from his mouth in that special voice he used only then, as if he were blessing them or consecrating himself. And then, for him, I didn't exist. Many, many, many times I didn't exist for him. But before a performance this exclusion – no, it wasn't an exclusion, it was an erasion – this erasion was absolute: he obliterated me. Me who tended him, humoured him, nursed him, sustained him – who debauched myself for him. Yes. That's the most persistent memory. Yes. And when I remember him like that in the back of the van, God how I hate him again –

    Kinlochbervie, Inverbervie,
    Inverdruie, Invergordon,
    Badachroo, Kinlochewe,
    Ballantrae, Inverkeithing,
    Cawdor, Kirkconnel,
    Plaidy, Kirkinner . . .

(*Quietly, almost dreamily*) Kinlochbervie's where the baby's buried, two miles south of the village, in a field on the left-hand side of the road as you go north. Funny, isn't it, but I've never met anybody who's been to Kinlochbervie, not even Scottish people. But it *is* a very small village and very remote, right away up in the north of Sutherland, about as far north as you can go in Scotland. And the people there told me that in good weather it is very beautiful and that you can see right across the sea to the Isle of Lewis in the Outer Hebrides. We just happened to be there and we were never back there again and the week that we were there it rained all the time, not really rained but a heavy wet mist so that you could scarcely see across the road. But I'm sure it is a beautiful place in good weather. Anyhow, that's where the baby's buried, in Kinlochbervie, in Sutherland, in the north of Scotland. Frank made a wooden cross to mark the grave and painted it white and wrote across it *Infant Child of Francis and Grace Hardy* – no name, of course, because it was still-born – just *Infant Child*. And I'm sure that cross is gone by now because it was a fragile thing and there were cows in the field and it wasn't a real cemetery anyway. And I had the baby in the back of the van and there was no nurse or doctor so no one knew anything about it except Frank and Teddy and me. And there was no clergyman at the graveside – Frank just said a few prayers that he made up. So there is no record of any kind. And he never talked about it afterwards; never once mentioned it again; and because he didn't, neither did I. So that was it. Over and done with. A finished thing. Yes. But I think it's a nice name, Kinlochbervie – a complete sound – a name you wouldn't forget easily . . . (*Tense again.*) God, he was such a twisted man! With such a talent for hurting. One of his mean tricks was to humiliate me by always changing my surname. It became Dodsmith or Elliot or O'Connell or McPherson – whatever came into his head; and I came from Yorkshire or Kerry or London or Scarborough or Belfast; and he had cured me of a blood disease; and

we weren't married – I was his mistress – always
that – that was the one constant: 'You haven't met
Gracie McClure, have you? She's my mistress,'
knowing so well that that would wound me and it
always did; it shouldn't have; I should have become
so used to it; but it always did. And Teddy – Teddy
wasn't just a fit-up man who was always in trouble
with the police for pilfering but a devoted servant,
dedicated acolyte to the holy man. It wasn't that he
was simply a liar – I never understood it – yes, I knew
that he wanted to hurt me, but it was much more
complex than that; it was some compulsion he had to
adjust, to refashion, to re-create everything around
him. Even the people who came to him – they weren't
just sick people who were confused and frightened
and wanted to be cured; no, no; to him they were . . .
yes, they were real enough, but not real as persons,
real as fictions, his fictions, extensions of himself that
came into being only because of him. And if he cured
a man, that man became for him a successful fiction
and therefore actually real, and he'd say to me
afterwards, 'Quite an interesting character that, wasn't
he? I knew that would work.' But if he didn't cure
him, the man was forgotten immediately, allowed to
dissolve and vanish as if he had never existed. Even
his father, and if he loved anyone he loved his father,
even he was constantly re-created, even after his
death. He was in fact a storeman in a factory in
Limerick – I met him once, a nice old man; but Frank
wasn't content with that – he made him a stonemason
and a gardener and a bus-driver and a guard and a
musician. It was as if – and I'm groping at this – but it
seemed to me that he kept remaking people according
to some private standard of excellence of his own, and

19

as his standards changed, so did the person. But I'm sure it was always an excellence, a perfection, that was the cause of his restlessness and the focus of it.

We were in Wales when he got word of his father's death. He went home alone. And when he came back he spoke of the death as if it had been his mother's. 'She passed away quietly,' he said. 'I don't know how father'll manage without her.' And the point was his mother had been dead for years when I first met him. Oh, he was a convoluted man.

The first day I went to the doctor, he was taking down all the particulars and he said to me, 'And what was your late husband's occupation, Mrs Hardy?' 'He was 'an artist,' I said – quickly – casually – but with complete conviction – just the way he might have said it. Wasn't that curious? Because the thought had never occurred to me before. And then because I said it and the doctor wrote it down, I knew it was true . . .

I left him once. Yes; I left *him*! Up and left. God, when I think of it! We'd been married seven years at the time, and within that twelve months I'd had a pleurisy and then two miscarriages in quick succession and I suppose I was feeling very sorry for myself. And we'd been living that winter in a derelict cottage in Norfolk miles from anyone – it was really a converted byre. I remember kneeling before a tiny grate and crying because the timber was so wet the fire wouldn't light, and trying to get to sleep on a damp mattress on the floor. Anyway we'd had a fight about something silly; and I must have been very depressed or suddenly worked myself up into a stupid panic because on some mad impulse I tore a page off an old calendar and wrote on the back of it, 'Dear Frank I'm leaving you because I cannot endure the depravity of our lives any

longer do not follow me I love you deeply Grace.'
Wasn't it awful! 'I love you deeply' – to a man like
that. And 'Do not follow me' – do not follow me! –
God, I had some kind of innocence then!

Anyhow I went home. For the first time and the last
time. I got the night-crossing from Glasgow and then
the bus to Omagh and walked the three miles out to
Knockmoyle. I remember I stood at the gates for a
while and looked up the long straight avenue flanked
with tall straight poplars, across the lawn, beyond the
formal Japanese garden and into the chaotic vegetable
plot where my mother messed about and devoted
her disturbed life to. It was Bridie, the housekeeper,
who reared me; and mother in her headscarf and
wellingtons was a strange woman who went in and
out of the mental hospital.

Father was in the breakfast-room, in a wicker chair
beside a huge fire, with a rug around his knees and his
head slightly forward and staring straight in front of
him just as he did when he was on the bench and
hectoring a defendant. The stroke had spared his
features and he looked so distinguished with his
patrician face and his white hair perfectly groomed
and his immaculate grey suit.

And I knocked on the table so that I wouldn't
startle him and I said, 'It's me, Father. It's Grace.'

'What's that? Speak up!'

And I could hear old Bridie moving about the
kitchen and I was afraid she'd hear me and come up
and throw her arms around me before I'd have a
chance to kiss him over and over again and say sorry
and tell him how often I thought about him.

I moved round so that I was directly in front of him.

'It's Grace, Father.'

'Yes? Yes?'

'Grace – Gracie.'

'Raise your voice. You're mumbling.'

'Timmikins,' I said – that's what he used to call me when I was a child.

'Who?'

'Timmikins,' I said again.

'I know who it is,' he said.

'I came home to see you,' I said.

He gazed at me for a long, long time. And his mouth opened and shut but no sound came. And then finally and suddenly the words and the remembrance came together for him.

'You ran off with the mountebank.' And he wasn't accusing – all he wanted was corroboration.

'Frank and I got married,' I said.

'Yes, you ran off with the mountebank just after you qualified. And you killed your mother – you know that. But I told her you'd be back. Six months, I said; give her six months and she'll come crawling back.'

I was crouching in front of him and holding his cold hands and our faces so close that I could smell his breath.

'Father,' I said, 'Father, listen –'

But words were now spilling out of him, not angry words but the tired formula words of the judge sentencing me to nine months in jail but suspending the sentence because he understood I came from a professional family with a long and worthy record of public service and hoping that I would soon regret and atone for the blemish I had brought on that family and on my own profession and threatening that if I ever appeared before him again he would have no option but to send me to jail and impose the maximum penalty et cetera, et cetera, et cetera.

And as I watched him and listened to him and felt the darts of his spittle on my face, I had an impulse – and I thank God I resisted it – a calm, momentary impulse to do an ugly, shameful thing: I wanted to curse him – no, not curse him – assault and defile him with obscenities and to articulate them slowly and distinctly and brutally into his patrician face; words he never used; a language he didn't speak; a language never heard in that house. But even in his confusion he'd understand it and recognise it as the final rejection of his tall straight poplars and the family profession and his formal Japanese gardens. But more important, much, much more important, recognise it as my proud testament to my mountebank and the van and the wet timber and the primus stove and the dirty halls and everything he'd call squalor. But thank God I didn't do that. Instead – and he was still sentencing me – I just walked away. And I never saw him again. And he died before the year was over. And the next night I was back in the Norfolk byre, back on the damp mattress and kissing Frank's face and shoulders and chest and telling him how sorry I was; and he's drunk and giving me his sly smile and saying little. And then I was pregnant again and this time I held on to it for the full time. And that was the black-faced, macerated baby that's buried in a field in Kinlochbervie in Sutherland in the north of Scotland –

Badrallach, Kilmore,
Llanfaethlu, Llanfechell,
Kincardine, Kinross,
Loughcarron, Lougligelly . . .

23

(*At banner*) Faith healer – faith healing – I never understood it, never. I tried to. In the beginning I tried diligently – as the doctor might say I brought all my mental rigour to bear on it. But I couldn't even begin to apprehend it – this gift, this craft, this talent, this art, this magic – whatever it was he possessed, that defined him, that was, I suppose, essentially him. And because it was his essence and because it eluded me I suppose I *was* wary of it. Yes, of course I was. And he knew it. Indeed, if by some miracle Frank could have been the same Frank without it, I would happily have robbed him of it. And he knew that, too – how well he knew that; and in his twisted way read into it the ultimate treachery on my part. So what I did was, I schooled myself – I tried to school myself – to leave it to him and him with it and be content to be outside them. And for a time that seemed to work for both of us: we observed the neutrality of the ground between us. But as time went on and particularly in the last few years when he became more frantic and more truculent, he began to interpret my remove as resentment, even as hostility, or he pretended he did – you could never be sure with him – and he insisted on dragging me into feud between himself and his talent. And then we would snarl and lunge and grapple at one another and things were said that should never have been said and that lay afterwards on our lives like slow poison. When his talent was working for him, the aggression wasn't quite so bitter – after he'd cured someone he'd be satisfied just to flaunt himself, to taunt me: 'And what does the legal mind make of all that? Just a con, isn't it? Just an illusion, isn't it?' And I'd busy myself putting away the chairs or taking down the banner. But when he couldn't perform – and in those last two years that became more and more frequent, the more desperate he became – then he'd go for me with bared teeth as if I were responsible and he'd scream at me, 'You were at your very best tonight, Miss O'Dwyer, weren't you? A great night for the law, wasn't it? You vengeful, spiteful bitch.' And I'd defend myself. And we'd tear one another apart.

As soon as we'd open the doors, that's where I'd take my seat, at a table if there was one, or if there wasn't, with a tray on my knee; because sometimes they'd pay on their way in, now and again far more than they could afford, I suppose in the hope that somehow it would sweeten Frank to them. And that's where I'd sit all through the performance and collect whatever they'd leave on the way out.

And when they'd all be seated – 'all'! Many a time we were lucky to have half a dozen – then Teddy'd put on the record, a worn-out hissing version of a song called 'The Way You Look Tonight'. I begged Frank to get something else, anything else. But he wouldn't. It had to be that. 'I like it,' he'd say, 'and it confuses them.'

Then Teddy'd come out and make his announcement.

And then Frank would appear.

I wish you could have seen him. It wasn't that he was a handsome man. He wasn't really. But when he came out before those people and moved among them and touched them – even though he was often half drunk – he had a special . . . magnificence. And I'd sit there and watch him and I'd often find myself saying to myself, 'Oh you lucky woman.' Oh, yes, oh, indeed, yes.

She sits and pours a drink.

I didn't want to come back to Ireland. Neither did Teddy. But he insisted. He had been in bad shape for months and although he didn't say it – he would never have said it – I knew he had some sense that Ireland might somehow recharge him, maybe even restore him. Because in that last year he seemed to have lost touch with his gift. And of course he was drinking too much and missing performances and picking fights with strangers – cornering someone in a pub and boasting that he could perform miracles and having people laugh at him; or else lying in the back of the van – we lived in it most of the time now – lying in the van and not speaking or eating for days.

But the real trouble was the faith healing. It wasn't that he didn't try – I suppose trying hadn't much to do with it anyway – but he tried too hard, he tried desperately, and usually nothing happened, nothing at all. I remember, just a few weeks before we came back, he met an old woman in an off-licence in Kilmarnock and he told her he could cure her arthritis. And he tried. And he failed. In the old days he wouldn't have given her another thought; but he became obsessed with that old woman, found out where she lived, went to her house again and again until finally her son-in-law threw him out and threatened to get the police for him.

So on the last day of August we crossed from Stranraer to Larne and drove through the night to County Donegal. And there we got lodgings in a pub, a lounge bar, really, outside a village called Ballybeg, not far from Donegal Town. (*She moves again.*) And the strange thing was that night began so well. I remember watching him and thinking: Yes, his sense was true, he is going to be restored here – he was so easy and so

relaxed and so charming, and there was nobody more
charming than him when he wanted to be. I could tell
even by the way he was drinking – not gulping down
the first three or four drinks as if they were only
preliminaries. And he chatted to the landlord and they
talked about the harvest and about fishing and about
the tourist trade. He even introduced me as his wife –
God, I suppose that ought to have alerted me.

And there was a group of young men in the lounge,
five of them, local men on their way home from their
friend's wedding; and one of them, the youngest of
them, was in a wheelchair. And they were sitting in a
corner by themselves and you could tell they wanted
to be left alone. And when I saw him go over to
them I had a second of unease. But whatever it was
he said to them, they smiled and shook hands with
him and moved into the centre of the lounge and he
called me over and we all sat round in a big circle and
one of them ordered a drink and the landlord joined
us and we just sat there and chatted and laughed
and told stories and sang songs. Where was Teddy?
(*remembering*) Yes, he was there, too, just outside the
circle, slightly drunk and looking a bit bewildered.
And it began as such a happy night – yes, happy,
happy, happy! The young men were happy. I was
happy. And Frank – yes, yes, I know he was happy
too. And then out of the blue – we were talking about
gambling – Frank suddenly leaned across to one of the
wedding guests, a young man called Donal, and said,
'I can cure that finger of yours.' And it was dropped
as lightly, as casually, as naturally into the conversation
as if he had said, 'This is my round.' So naturally that
the others didn't even hear it and went on talking.
And he caught the twisted finger between his palms

and massaged it gently and then released it and the
finger was straight and he turned immediately to me
and gave me an icy, exultant, theatrical smile and said,
'That's the curtain-raiser.'

And I knew at once – I knew it instinctively – that
before the night was out he was going to measure
himself against the cripple in the wheelchair.

And he did. Yes. Outside in the yard. I watched
from an upstairs window. But that was hours later,
just after daybreak. And throughout the night the
others had become crazed with drink and he had gone
very still and sat with his eyes half-closed but never
for a second taking them off the invalid.

Before they all went out to the yard – it was almost
dawn then – I gripped him by the elbow. 'For Christ's
sake, Frank, please, for my sake,' and he looked at me,
no, not at me, not at me, past me, beyond me, out of
those damn benign eyes of his; and I wasn't there for
him . . .

Aberarder, Kinlochbervie,

Aberayron, Kinlochbervie,

Invergordon, Kinlochbervie . . . in Sutherland, in
the north of Scotland . . .

(by rote) But I *am* getting stronger. I *am* becoming more
controlled. I can measure my progress by the number
of hours I sleep and the amount I drink and – and –

O my God I'm in such a mess – I'm really in such
a mess – how I want that door to open – how I want
that man to come across that floor and put his white
hands on my face and still this tumult inside me –
O my God I'm one of his fictions too, but I need him
to sustain me in that existence – O my God I don't
know if I can go on without his sustenance.

Fade to black.

Part Three

TEDDY

We discover Teddy on stage. He is probably in his
fifties but it would be difficult to pinpoint his age
accurately because he has a showman's verve and
perkiness that make him appear younger than that.

He is wearing a bow-tie, checked shirt, smoking
jacket/dressing gown (short), house slippers.

We discover him sitting beside the table – the same
small table as in Part Two; but Teddy's chair is more
comfortable than Grace's. He is listening to a recording
of Fred Astaire singing 'The Way You Look Tonight' –
an old record-player and a very abused record.

Occasionally during his monologue he goes to a
small locker – like a hospital locker – where he keeps
his bottles of beer. Beside this locker is an empty
dog-basket.

The poster is in the same position as in Part One
and Part Two.

(No attempt has been made to write this monologue
in the phonetic equivalent of Cockney/London English.
But the piece must be played in that dialect.)

Teddy is sitting with his eyes closed, his head back,
listening to the music.

> Some day when I'm awf'ly low
> When the world is cold,
> I will feel a glow
> Just thinking of you
> And the way you look tonight . . .

At the end of the first verse he opens his eyes, sees
that his glass is empty, goes to the locker, gets a bottle
of beer and comes back to his seat. Omit all the
middle verses – go from the first verse to the last. As
Teddy gets his drink he sings odd lines with the
record.

> Lovely, never, never change,
> Keep that breathless charm,
> Won't you please arrange it
> 'Cause I love you
> Just the way you look tonight.
> Mm, mm, mm, mm,
> Just the way you look tonight.

Teddy What about that then, eh? Fred Astaire.
Fantastic, isn't it? One of the greats, Freddy. Just
fantastic. I could listen to that all day – (*Sings.*) 'Just
the way you look . . .' It was Gracie insisted on that
for our theme music. And do you know why, dear
heart? She wouldn't admit it to him but she told me.
Because that was the big hit the year she and Frank
was married. Can you imagine! But of course as time
goes by she forgets that. And of course he never knows
why it's our theme – probably thinks I've got some sort
of a twisted mind. So that the two of them end up
blaming *me* for picking it! But by that time I really like
the tune, you know; and anyway it's the only record
we have. So I keep it. And old Teddy, he's the only one
of the three of us that knows its romantic significance.
I'll tell you something, dear heart: spend your life in
show-business and you become a philosopher.

But it is a fantastic tune, isn't it? Did you ever look
back over all the great artists – old Freddy here, Lillie
Langtry, Sir Laurence Olivier, Houdini, Charlie Chaplin,

Gracie Fields – and did you ever ask yourself what makes them all top-liners, what have they all got in common? Okay, I'll tell you. Three things. Number one: they've got ambition this size. Okay? Number two: they've got a talent that is sensational and unique – there's only one Sir Laurence – right? Number three: not one of them has two brains to rub together. You think I'm joking? I promise you. They know they have something fantastic, sure, they're not that stupid. But what it is they have, how they do it, how it works, what that sensational talent is, what it all means – believe me, they don't know and they don't care and even if they did care they haven't the brains to analyse it.

Let me tell you about two dogs I had once. Okay? One was a white poodle and she was so brilliant – I mean, that dog, she knew what you were thinking about before you even thought about it yourself. Before I'd come home at night, d'you know what that dog would do? She'd switch on the electric fire, pull the curtains, and leave my slippers and a bottle of beer sitting there beside my chair. But put her in front of an audience – fell apart – couldn't do nothing. Right. Now the other dog he was a whippet. Maybe you remember him, Rob Roy, the Piping Dog?

Brief pause.

Well, it was quite a few years ago. Anyway, you see that whippet, he was fantastic. I mean to say, just tell me how many times in your life has it been your privilege to hear a three-year-old male whippet dog play 'Come into the Garden, Maud' on the bagpipes *and* follow for his encore with 'Plaisir d'Amour'. Okay? Agreed. Sensational talent. Ambition? I couldn't stop him rehearsing. Morning, noon and night he'd sit there blowing the bloody thing and working them bellows with his back leg – all night long if I'd let him. That's all he lived for, being on top of the heap. And brains? Had he brains, that whippet? Let me tell you. I had that dog four and a half years, until he expired from pulmonary exhaustion. And in all that time that whippet couldn't even learn his name! I mean it. I mean apart from his musical genius that whippet in human terms was educationally subnormal. A retarded whippet, in fact. I'd stub my toe against something, and I'd say 'God!', and who'd come running to me, wagging his tail? I tell you: a philosopher – that's what you become.

I'll give you another example. One of the best acts I ever handled – Miss Mulatto and Her Pigeons. You see that kid? D'you know what that kid could do? I swear to God this is no lie, that kid talked pigeon! I swear. Fluent. That kid could plant her pigeons all over the house – some here, some there, some down there; and then she'd stand in the centre of the stage and she'd speak to them in a great flood of pigeon, you know – I can't do it, I can't even speak English – but this flood of pigeon would come out of her. And suddenly all those birds – a hundred and twenty of them, I should know, six to a box, twenty boxes, that's when I had to buy the van – all those birds would rise up from all over the house and come flying in like a bloody massive snowstorm and smother her on the stage. Fantastic. Can you imagine it? Her being able to talk to every one of them hundred and twenty birds and for all I know maybe them all speaking different languages! I said to her once, 'Mary Brigid,' I said, that was her name, Mary Brigid O'Donnell, I said, 'What do you say to them?' And she tossed her head and she said, 'Say to them? How would I know what I say to them, Teddy? I just make sounds at them.' See?

He touches his head.

Nothing. Empty. But what a talent! What an artist! And another thing, when those birds all died that winter of '47 – all of them, just like that, within twenty-four hours, we were in Crewe at the time, the vet said it was galloping shingles – after those birds died, Mary Brigid never worked again. I suppose it'd be like as if . . . as if someone sat on Yehudi Menuhin's fiddle and smashed it. God! Bloody artists!

Teddy disposes of the empty bottle and sings as he does.

Oh, but you're lovely
With your smile so warm,
And your cheek so soft
There is nothing for me but to love you –

I'll tell you something: if you're thinking of going into the promotion business, let me tell you something – I'll give you this for nothing – it's the best advice you'll ever get – and it has been the one ruling principle in all my years as a professional man: if you're going to handle great artists, you must handle them – believe me, I know what I'm talking about – you must handle them on the basis of a relationship that is strictly business only. Personally, in the privacy of your heart, you may love them or you may hate them. But that has nothing to do with it. Your client he has his job to do. You have your job to do. On that basis you complement each other. But let that relationship between you spill over into friendship or affection and believe me, dear heart, the coupon's torn. The one rule I've always lived by: friends is friends and work is work, and as the poet says, never the twain shall meet. Okay? Okay. (*indicating poster*) Him? No, he was no great artist. Course he was no great artist. Never anything more than a mediocre artist. At best. Believe me. I should know, shouldn't I? Sure he had talent. Talent? He had more talent – listen to me – he had more talent than – and brains? – brains! – that's all the stupid bastard had was brains! For Christ's sake, brains! And what did they do for him, I ask you, all those bloody brains? They bloody castrated him – that's what they done for him – bloody knackered him! So what do you end up handling? A bloody fantastic talent that hasn't one ounce of ambition because his bloody brains has him bloody castrated! Tell me – go ahead – you tell me – you tell me – I genuinely want to know – what sort of act is that to work with, to spend your life with? How do you handle an act like that? You tell *me*. I never knew! I never learned! Oh, for God's sake, no wonder I have ulcers!

Pause. Then softly:

But when his brain left him alone. When he was in form.

There was one night in particular. Wales it was. Village called Llanblethian. An old Methodist church that I get for ten bob. A week before Christmas.

And we're flat broke. And Frank, he's on two bottles of whiskey a day at this stage. And Gracie and him they've been fighting something terrible and she's disappeared off somewhere. And I've a pocketful of bills to pay.

Okay. Eight o'clock. I open the doors. I'm not exactly knocked down in the stampede. As a matter of

34

fact, dear heart – nobody. God. And now it's snowing.
I close the doors. Frank, he's looking like he's about to
die, and his hands and his shoulders they're shaking
like this. 'Get me a drink,' he says. I pretend I don't
hear him. The door's flung open. The stampede? (*He
shakes his head.*) Gracie. 'Where's the genius?' she
shouts. 'I came to see the great Irish genius. Where is
he?' And he hears her and he screams, 'Get that bitch
out! Get rid of that bitch!' 'Oh, he's here, is he?' she
says. 'Physician, heal thyself!' she says with this great,
mad, mocking voice. 'Out! Out!' he shouts. 'The
genius!' she screams. 'Out! Out!' 'Genius!' And their
voices they're echoing up through those dirty big oak
rafters of the church so that it goes on and on and
on . . . Oh, God, I mean to say, dear heart . . .

Finally – it must be near nine o'clock now – we're
about to pack up and the door opens and in come ten
people. I don't remember all the details now. There's
two kids, I know; one of them has this great big lump
on his cheek. And there's a woman with crutches.
And there's another young woman with a crying baby
in her arms. And there's a young man with dark
glasses and one of those white sticks for blind people.
Five or six others – I can't remember – I mean I didn't
know then the kind of night it was going to be, did I?
Oh, yes, and an old man, a farmer – he's lame – he's
helped in by his daughter. And they all sit down.
And I goes through my paces: Ladies and gentlemen
and etcetera and so on. And then I goes to Frank and
I says, 'Okay, Frank?' And very slowly he straightens
up and when I see his face I'm sure he's going to be
sick and he doesn't answer me at all but sort of –
you know – drifts past me and down to them and
among them.

He slowly pours the remains of a bottle into his glass. Then takes a drink.

All I can say now is that it was . . . I mean I don't ask you to believe what happened. Quite honestly – and I don't say this with no belligerence – it makes no difference to me whether you believe me or not. But what happened that night in that old Methodist hall in the village of Llanbethian in Glamorganshire in Wales is that every single person in that church was cured. Ten people. All made right again. I'd seen him do fantastic things before but I'd never seen him do anything on that scale. Never. And I'll tell you a funny thing: there was no shouting or cheering or dancing with joy, nothing at all like that. Hardly a word was spoken. It was like as if not only had he taken away whatever it was was wrong with them, but like he had given them some great content in themselves as well. That sounds silly, doesn't it? But that's the way it seemed.

And when he had finished, they all got to their feet and shook his hand, one after the other, very formal like. And the old farmer, the one who'd been lame and had been helped in by his daughter, he made a little speech. He said, in that lilting Welsh accent – I can't do that neither – he said, 'Mr Hardy, as long as men live in Glamorganshire, you'll be remembered here.' And whatever way he said it, you knew it was true; and whatever way he said Glamorganshire, it sounded like the whole world. And then he took out his wallet and placed it on the table and he said, 'I hope I'm not insulting you, sir.' And they all went out.

Short pause.

36

That was one of the big nights, that was. I mean we were stunned – Gracie – me – Frank himself; we just stood looking at one another. I mean to say – ten people – all in a few minutes. And then he suddenly went crazy with delight. And he threw his arms around me and kissed me on both cheeks. And then he ran down to Gracie and caught her in his arms and lifted her up into the air and danced her up and down the aisle of that old church and the two of them sang at the top of their voices, 'Lovely, never never change', trying to sing and dance and at the same time breaking their sides laughing. And then he flung the doors open and they ran outside and sang and danced in the snow. What a pair! Oh my dear, what a pair! Like kids they were. Just like kids. Then I heard the van starting up. But by the time I got out they were gone. Just like that. Didn't see them again for four days – what happened was they went off to some posh hotel in Cardiff and lived it up until the wallet was empty. Just like kids, you know. Thoughtless; no thought for tomorrow. And no cruelty intended – oh no, no cruelty. But at a time like that a bit thoughtless. And that's understandable, too, after a night like that, isn't it? just a little bit thoughtless – that's all.

He goes to the locker for another bottle. As he goes:

What a funny couple they were, though. Oh dear, what a funny couple. I mean to spend the greater part of their lives together, fighting as they did; and when I say fighting, I mean really sticking the old knife in and turning it as hard as they could. I never understood it – job for the head-shrink, isn't it? – why two people should burn themselves out in that way. Sure they could have split. Why didn't they then? Don't ask me. For God's sake why didn't I leave them and get myself something nice and simple and easy like – like – like a whistling dolphin? And what was the fighting all about in the end? All right you could say it was because the only thing that finally mattered to him was his work – and that would be true. Or you could say it was because the only thing that finally mattered to her was him – and I suppose that would be true, too. But when you put the two propositions together like that – I don't know – somehow they both become only half-truths, you know.

Or maybe you could say that no artist should ever be married. I've heard that theory, too; and after a lifetime in the profession I would incline to the conclusion that that theory has quite a bit of validity in it. I mean look at Rob Roy, the Piping Dog. just consider for one minute the fortune I could have made in stud fees when that dog was a household name. Queuing up with their bitches they were; queuing bloody up. Twenty nicker a throw they were offering me. I thought I was sitting on a gold-mine. Do you know what I did in anticipation of the fortune that was going to come pouring in? I got a fifteen-foot black Carrara marble headstone with gold lettering put up over my mother's grave. Set me back £214, that did. Okay – and what happened? – what happened every single time? I'll tell you. I come into the room here with a very beautiful and very sexy whippet bitch. He's just been rehearsing and he's lying there in that basket, gasping for breath. I say to him, 'Look at this then, old Rob. Who's good to you then, eh?' But he's temperamental – he won't look up. And the bitch, she's rolling her eyes and waggling all over

and laughing like a bloody gypsy. 'Come on, boy,'
I say, 'come on, come on. You've got a nice friend
here.' And what does he do every time, every single
time? He gets to his feet. He gives this great yawn. And
then suddenly – just like that – goes for her throat!
For her bloody *throat* for God's sake! Tries to tear her
limb from bloody limb! Course he's stupid but he's
not that stupid! I mean he knows what it's all about!
My God he knows! My God, there's days he's so
randy, that whippet, there's days I daren't strap the
bloody bagpipes to him! And yet look what he does
when it's bloody handed to him on a plate – some of
the most beautiful whippet bitches in the country and
every one of them crying out for it! Goes for her
throat and tries to desecrate my mother's memory at
the same time! Oh my God – artists! I ask you!

   *He gathers the empty bottles on the table and drops
   them into a waste-paper basket. As he does:*

Ups and downs – losses and gains – roundabouts and
swings – isn't that it?
   And if that night in Llanbethian was one of the
high spots, I suppose the week we spent in that village
in Sutherland was about as bad a patch as we ever
struck. For Gracie it was. Certainly for Gracie. And
for me, too, I think. Oh, that's going back a fair few
years. About the time he really began to lose control
of the drinking. Anyway, there we were away up in
Sutherland – what *was* the name of that village?
Inverbuie? Inverbervie? Kinlochbervie? – that's it! –
Kinlochbervie! – very small, very remote, right away
up in the north of Sutherland, about as far north as
you can go in Scotland, and looking across at the Isle
of Lewis in the Outer Hebrides.

I'll always remember our first sight of that village. We climb up this long steep hill through this misty fog and when we get to the top we stop; and away down below us in the valley – there's Kinlochbervie; and it is just bathed in sunshine. First time we've seen the sun in about a month. And now here's this fantastic little village sitting on the edge of the sea, all blue and white and golden, and all lit up and all sparkling and all just heavenly. And Gracie she turns to me and she says, 'Teddy,' she says, 'this is where my baby'll be born.' Even though she wasn't due for three more weeks. But she was right. That's where the baby was born.

Okay. We head down into the valley and just about two miles out of the village the front axle goes thrackk! Terrific. Frank, he's out cold in the back. So I leave Gracie sunbathing herself on a stone wall and I hikes it into Kinlochbervie to get help.

That was a Tuesday morning. The following Friday we're still there, still waiting for a local fisherman called Campbell who's out in his trawler to come back 'cause he's the only local who owns a tractor and we're depending on his mother who happens to be deaf as a post to persuade him when he comes back to tow us the thirty-five miles to the nearest village where there's a blacksmith but there's a chance, too, that this blacksmith might not be at home when we get there because his sister, Annie, she's getting married to a postman in Glasgow and the blacksmith may be the best man. One of those situations – you know. (*Shouts.*) 'Are you sure this blacksmith can fix axles, dear heart?' 'Och, Annie, she's a beautiful big strong girl with brown eyes.'

Right. We hang about. And since funds are low – as usual – Gracie and Frank they sleep in the van and

I'm kipping in a nearby field. I don't mind; the weather's beautiful. Saturday passes – no Campbell. Sunday passes – no Campbell. And then on Sunday evening . . . the baby's born.

Very slowly he goes for another beer, opens it, pours it. As he does this he whistles a few lines of 'The Way You Look Tonight' through his teeth. Then with sudden anger:

Christ, you've got to admit he really was a bastard in many ways! I know he was drinking heavy – I know – I know all that! But for Christ's sake to walk away deliberately when your wife's going to have your baby in the middle of bloody nowhere – I mean to say, to do that deliberately, that's some kind of bloody-mindedness, isn't it? And make no mistake, dear heart: it was deliberate, it was bloody-minded. 'Cause as soon as she starts having the pains, I go looking for him, and there he is heading up the hill, and I call after him, and I know he hears me, but he doesn't answer me. Oh, Christ, there really was a killer instinct deep down in that man!

Pause. He takes a drink, puts the glass down on the table and looks at it.

I don't know . . . I don't know how we managed. God, when I think of it. Her lying on my old raincoat in the back of the van . . . shouting for him, screaming for him . . . all that blood . . . her bare feet pushing, kicking against my shoulders . . . 'Frank!' she's screaming, 'Frank! Frank!' and I'm saying, 'My darling, he's coming – he's coming, my darling – he's on his way – he'll be here any minute' . . . and then that – that little wet thing with the black face and the

black body, a tiny little thing, no size at all . . . a boy
it was . . .

Pause.

And afterwards she was so fantastic – I mean she was
so bloody fantastic. She held it in her arms, just sitting
there on the roadside with her back leaning against
the stone wall and her legs stretched out in front of
her, just sitting there in the sun and looking down at
it in her arms. And then after about half an hour she
said, 'It's time to bury it now, Teddy.' And we went
into a nearby field and I had to chase the cows away
'cause they kept following us and I dug the hole and
I put it in the hole and I covered it up again. And then
she asked me was I not going to say no prayers over
it and I said sure, why not, my darling, I said; but not
being much of a praying man I didn't know right
what to say; so I just said this was the infant child
of Francis Hardy, Faith Healer, and his wife, Grace
Hardy, both citizens of Ireland, and this was where
their infant child lies, in Kinlochbervie, in Sutherland;
and God have mercy on all of us, I said.

And all the time she was very quiet and calm. And
when the little ceremony was concluded, she put her
two white hands on my face and brought me to her
and kissed me on the forehead. Just once. On the
forehead.

And later that evening I made a cross and painted
it white and placed it on top of the grave. Maybe it's
still there. You never know. About two miles south of
the village of Kinlochbervie. In a field on the left-hand
side of the road as you go north. Maybe it's still there.
Could well still be. Why not? Who's to say?

Pause.

Oh, he came back all right; just before it was dark.
Oh, sure. Sober as a judge, all spruced up, healthy-
looking, sunburned, altogether very cocky; and full
of old chat to me about should we have a go in the
Outer Hebrides or maybe we should cross over to the
east coast or should we plan a journey even further
north now that the weather was so good – you know,
all business, things he never gave a damn about. And
he seemed so – you know – so on top of things, I
thought for a while, I thought: My God, he doesn't
know! He genuinely doesn't know! But then suddenly
in the middle of all this great burst of interest I see
him glancing into the van with the corner of the eye –
not that there was anything to see; I had it all washed
out by then – but it was the way he done it and the
way he kept on talking at the same time that I *knew*
that *he* knew; and not only that he knew but that he
knew it all right down to the last detail. And even
though the old chatter never faltered for a minute,
whatever way he kept talking straight into my face,
I knew too that – oh, I don't know how to put it –
but I got this feeling that in a kind of way – being the
kind of man he was – well somehow I got the feeling,
I *knew* that he *had* to keep talking because he had
suffered all that she had suffered and that now he
was . . . about to collapse. Yeah. Funny, wasn't it?
And many a time since then I get a picture of him
going up that hill that Sunday afternoon, like there's
some very important appointment he's got to keep,
walking fast with his head down and pretending he
doesn't hear me calling him. And I've thought maybe –
course it was bloody minded of him! I'm not denying

that! – but maybe being the kind of man he was, you know, with that strange gift he had, I've thought maybe – well, maybe he had to have his own way of facing things . . .

Oh, I don't know. None of my business, was it? None of my concern, thank the Lord, except in so far as it might affect the performance of my client. Listen to me, dear heart, I'll give you this for nothing, the best advice you'll ever get – the *one* rule I've always lived by: friends is friends and work is work and never the twain shall meet as the poet says. Okay? Okay.

> *With a glass in his hand he goes slowly upstage until he is standing beneath the poster. As he goes he hums the lines 'Some day when I'm awf'ly low, When the world is cold'. He reads:*

The Fantastic Francis Hardy, Faith Healer: One Night Only. Nice poster though, isn't it? A lifetime in the business and that's the only memento I've kept. That's a fact. See some people in our profession? – they hoard everything: press-clippings, posters, notices, photographs, interviews – they keep them all. Never believed in that, though. I mean the way I look at it, you've got to be a realist, you know, live in the present. Look at Sir Laurence – you think he spends his days poring over old albums? No, we don't have time for that. And believe me I've had my share of triumphs and my share of glory over the years; and I'm grateful for that. But I mean it doesn't butter no parsnips for me today, does it?

And do you know, dear heart, it was almost thrown out! Well, I mean it *was* thrown out – I just happened to spot it in this pile of stuff that Gracie's landlord had dumped outside for the dustmen. I'd come straight from the morgue in Paddington, and the copper there, he'd given me her address; and there I was, walking along the street, looking for Number 27; and there it is, lying on the footpath where her landlord had dumped it. I mean, if it had been raining, it would have been destroyed, wouldn't it? But there it was, neat as you like. And just as I was picking it up, this city gent, he's walking past and he says, 'How dare you steal private property, sir!' (*in a fury*) And I caught him by the neck and I put my fist up to his face and I said to him, I said to him, 'You open your fucking mouth once more, mate, just once fucking more, and I'll fucking well make fucking sausage meat of you!'

Pause while he controls himself again.

If you'll pardon the language, dear heart. But I just went berserk. I mean half an hour before, this copper he'd brought me to Paddington and I'm still in a state of shock after that. And besides it's only – what? – twelve months since the whole County Donegal thing: that night in the Ballybeg pub and then hanging about waiting for the trial of those bloody Irish Apaches and nobody in the courtroom understands a word I'm saying – they had to get an interpreter to explain to the judge in English what the only proper Englishman in the place was saying! God!

And I'm still only getting over all that when this copper comes up here one morning while I'm shaving and I opens the door and he asks me my name and I tell him and then he says I'm to go to Paddington with him right away to . . .

He stops suddenly and stares for a long time at the audience. Then:

45

Tell you what – why don't I go back twelve months and tell you first about that night in Ballybeg? Why don't I do that? Why not?

He gets another bottle, opens it, pours it.

It was the last day of August and we crossed from Stranraer to Larne and drove through the night to County Donegal. And there we got lodgings in a pub, a lounge bar, really, outside a village called Ballybeg, not far from Donegal Town.

He takes a drink and leaves the glass down. Pause.

You see that night in that pub in Ballybeg? You know how I spent that night? I spent the whole of that night just watching them. Mr and Mrs Frank Hardy. Side by side. Together in Ireland. At home in Ireland. Easy; relaxed; chatting; laughing. And it was like as if I was seeing them for the first time in years and years – no! not seeing them but *remembering them*. Funny thing that, wasn't it? I'm not saying they were strangers to me – strangers! I mean, Frank and Gracie, how could they be strangers to *me*! – but it was like as if I was seeing them as they were once, as they might have been all the time – like if there was never none of the bitterness and the fighting and the wettings and the bloody van and the smell of the primus stove and the bills and the booze and the dirty halls and that hassle that we never seemed to be able to rise above. Like away from all that, all that stuff cut out, this is what they could be.

And there they were, the centre of that big circle round that big lounge, everybody wanting to talk to them, them talking to everybody, now and then exchanging an odd private word between themselves, now and then even touching each other very easy and very casual.

And she was sitting forward in this armchair. And she was all animation and having a word with everybody and laughing all the time. And she was wearing this red dress. And her hair it was tied back with a black ribbon. And how can I tell you how fantastic she looked?

And then sometime around midnight someone said, 'Why don't you sing us a song, Gracie?' And as natural as you like, as if she done it every day of the week, she stood up and she sang an Irish song called 'Believe me if all those endearing young charms/Which I gaze on so fondly today'. Christ, I don't mean that's the title; that's the whole first verse for Christ's sake. And it wasn't that she was a sensational singer – no, no, she wasn't. I mean she had this kind of very light, wavery kind of voice – you know, like the voice of a kid of ten or eleven. But she stands up there in that Irish pub, in that red dress and with her hair all back from her face; and she's looking at him as she's singing; and we're all looking at her; and the song – it sort of comes out of her very simple and very sweet, like in a way not as if she's performing but as if the song's just sort of rising out of her by itself. And I'm sitting there just outside the circle, sitting there very quiet, very still. And I'm saying to myself, 'O Jesus, Teddy boy . . . Oh my Jesus . . . What are you going to do?'

And then I looks over at Frank – I mean I just happen to look over, you know the way you do – and there he is, gazing across at me. And the way he's gazing at me and the look he has on his face is exactly the way he looks into somebody he knows he's going to cure. I don't know – it's a hard thing to explain

47

if you've never seen it. It's a very serious look and it's a very compassionate look. It's a look that says two things. It says: No need to speak – I know exactly what the trouble is. And at the same time it says: I am now going to cure you of that trouble. That's the look he gave me. He held me in that look for – what? – thirty seconds. And then he turned away from me and looked at her – sort of directed his look towards her so that I had to look at her too. And suddenly she is this terrific woman that of course I love very much, married to this man that I love very much – love maybe even more. But that's all. Nothing more. That's all. And that's enough.

And for the first time in twenty years I was so content – so content, dear heart, do you know what I done? I got drunk in celebration – slowly, deliberately, happily slewed! And someone must have carried me upstairs to bed because the next thing I know Gracie's hammering on my chest and shouting and sobbing, 'Get up, Teddy! Get up! Something terrible has happened! Something horrible!'

Long pause as he goes and gets another beer.

But I was telling you about the poster and how it's lying on the street outside Gracie's digs. That's it. How I've just come from Paddington and how the copper he's given me her address. That's right – I've told you all that. Or to go back to the morning of that same day – twelve months exactly after that night in Ballybeg.

Okay. I'm shaving. Knock at the door. This copper. Asks me my name. I tell him. Asks me to come with him to the morgue in Paddington to identify a body. What body? Body of a lady. And I say what lady?

And he says a Mrs Grace Hardy. And I say come off it, she's in Ireland, that's where I left her. And he says you must be mistaken, she's been in London for the past four months, living in digs in Number 27, Limewood Avenue. Limewood Avenue! I mean this here is Limewood Grove! Limewood Avenue's just four streets away. And I say she's there now, is she? And he says no, she's dead, she's in the morgue. And I say you must be wrong, copper. And he says no mistake, she's dead, from an overdose of sleeping tablets, and would I come with him please and make a formal identification.

So the copper he brought me in a van to Paddington – you know, just like our van; only his van I'm sure it's taxed and insured. But it's the same inside: two seats in the front, me driving, her beside me, and Frank in the back all hunched up with the bottle between his legs. And there she was. Gracie all right. Looking very beautiful. Oh my dear I can't tell you how beautiful she looked.

And the copper he said, 'Is that Grace Hardy?' 'It is,' I said. 'Did you know her well?' 'Oh, yes,' I said, 'a professional relationship going back twenty-odd years.' 'Cause that's what it was, wasn't it, a professional relationship? Well it certainly wasn't nothing more than that, I mean, was it?

He stands for some seconds just looking at the audience. Then he does not see them any more. He sits on his chair and puts on the record. After the first few lines fade rapidly to black.

Part Four

FRANK

*The poster is gone. The set is empty except for the
single chair across which lies Frank's coat exactly as
he left it in Part One.*

*We discover Frank standing downstage left, where
we left him.*

*In this final section Frank is slightly less aloof,
not quite as detached as in Part One. To describe
him now as agitated would be a gross exaggeration.
But there should be tenuous evidence of a slightly
heightened pulse-rate, of something approximating to
excitement in him, perhaps in the way his mind leaps
without apparent connection from thought to thought;
and his physical movements are just a shade sharper.*

Frank (*eyes shut*)
  Aberarder, Kinlochbervie,
  Aberayron, Kinlochbervie,
  Invergordon, Kinlochbervie . . . in Sutherland, in
the north of Scotland . . .

  *He opens his eyes. A very brief pause. Then,
  recovering quickly:*

But I've told you all that, haven't I? – how we were
holidaying in Kinlochbervie when I got word that my
mother had died? Yes, of course I have. I've told you
all that. (*Begins moving.*) A picturesque little place,
very quiet, very beautiful, looking across to the Isle

of Lewis . . . about as far north as you can go in . . .
in Scotland . . .

*He keeps moving. As he does he searches his
pockets. Produces a newspaper clipping, very
tattered, very faded.*

I carried this around with me for years. A clipping from
the *West Glamorgan Chronicle*. 'A truly remarkable
event took place in the old Methodist church in
Llanblethian on the night of December 21st last when
an itinerant Irish faith healer called Francis Harding . . .'
For some reason they never seemed to – (*He shrugs in
dismissal.*) '. . . cured ten local people of a variety of
complaints ranging from blindness to polio. Whether
these very astonishing cures were effected by auto-
suggestion or whether Mr Harding is indeed the
possessor of some extra-terrestrial power . . .' Nice
word that. '. . . we are not as yet in a position to
adjudicate. But our preliminary investigations would
indicate that something of highly unusual proportions
took place that night in Llanblethian.'

'Unusual proportions' . . . (*Short laugh.*)

Never knew why I kept it for so long. Its testimony?
I don't think so. Its reassurance? No, not that. Maybe,
I think . . . maybe just as an identification. Yes, I think
that's why I kept it. It identified me – even though it
got my name wrong.

Yes, that *was* a strange night. One of those rare
nights when I could – when I could have moved
mountains. Ten people – one after the other. And only
one of them came back to thank me – an old farmer
who was lame. I remember saying to Gracie the next
day, 'Where are the other nine?' – in fun, of course;

of course in fun. But she chose to misunderstand me and that led to another row.

Yes; carried it for years; until we came back to Ireland. And that night in that pub in Ballybeg I crumpled it up (*He does this now.*) and threw it away.

I never met her father, the judge. Shortly after Gracie and I ran off together, he wrote me a letter; but I never met him. He said in it – the only part I remember – he used the phrase 'implicating my only child in your career of chicanery'. And I remember being angry and throwing the letter to her; and I remember her reading that line aloud and collapsing on the bed with laughing and kicking her heels in the air and repeating the phrase over and over again – I suppose to demonstrate her absolute loyalty to me. And I remember thinking how young she *did* look and how cruel her laughter at him was. Because by then my anger against him had died and I had some envy of the man who could use the word 'chicanery' with such confidence.

I would have liked to have had a child. But she was barren. And anyhow the life we led wouldn't have been suitable. And he might have had the gift. And he might have handled it better than I did. I wouldn't have asked for anything from him – love, affection, respect – nothing like that. But I would have got pleasure just in looking at him. Yes. A child would have been something. What is a piece of paper? Or those odd moments of awe, of gratitude, of adoration? Nothing, nothing, nothing . . .

(*Looking around*) It was always like this – shabby, shabby, bleak, derelict. We never got that summons to Teddy's royal palace; not even to a suburban drawing-room. And it would have been interesting to have been just once – not for the pretensions, no, no, but to discover was it possible in conditions other than these, just for the confirmation that this despair, this surrender wasn't its own healing. Yes, that would have been interesting.

And yet . . . and yet . . .

(*Suddenly, rapidly*) Not for a second, not for a single second was I disarmed by the warmth and the camaraderie and the deference and the joviality and the joy and the effusion of that home-coming welcome that night in that pub in Ballybeg. No, not for a second. Of course I responded to it. Naturally I responded to it. And yes, the thought did cross my mind that at long last is there going to be – what? – a fulfilment, an integration, a full blossoming? Yes, that thought occurred to me. But the moment that boy Donal threatened me with his damned twisted finger, that illusion quickly vanished. And I knew, I knew instinctively why I was being hosted.

Aberarder, Kinlochbervie,
Aberayron, Kinlochbervie,
Invergordon, Kinlochbervie . . .

Where had we got to? Ah, yes – Teddy had been put to bed and Gracie had finished her housekeeping – I could hear her moving about upstairs; and the wedding guests had gone to get McGarvey. Only the landlord and myself in that huge, garish lounge.

I walked around it for a time.

I thought of Teddy asleep upstairs, at peace and reconciled at last. And I wondered had I held on to him out of selfishness, should I have attempted to release him years ago. But I thought – no; his passion was a sustaining one. And maybe, indeed, maybe I had impoverished him now.

And I thought of Gracie's mother and the one time we met, in Dublin, on her way back to hospital. We were in a restaurant together, the three of us, Gracie and she and I; and she never spoke until Gracie had gone off to pay the bill and then she said, 'I suffer from nerves, you know,' her face slightly averted from me but looking directly at me at the same time and smiling at me. I said I knew. I was afraid she was going to ask me for help. 'What do you make of that?' I said I was sure she would get better this time. 'You know, there are worse things,' she said. I said I knew that. 'Much, much worse,' she went on and she was almost happy-looking now. 'Look at her father – he is obsessed with order. That's worse.' I suppose so, I said. 'And Grace – she wants devotion, and that's worse still.' 'Is it?' I asked. 'And what do you want?' And before I could answer, Gracie came back, and the smile vanished, and the head dropped. And that was all. No request for help. And I never heard her voice again.

And I remembered – suddenly, for no reason at all – the day my father took me with him to the horse fair in Ballinasloe. And the only incident I remembered was that afternoon, in a pub. And a friend of my father's, Eamon Boyle, was with us; and the two men were slightly drunk. And Boyle put his hand on my head and said to my father, 'And what's this young man going to be, Frank?' And my father opened his mouth and laughed and said, 'Be Jaysus, Boyle, it'll be hard for him to beat his aul fella!' And for the first time I saw his mouth was filled with rotten teeth. And I remember being ashamed in case Boyle had seen them, too. Just a haphazard memory. Silly. Nothing to it. But for some reason it came back to me that night.

And I thought of the first big row Grace and I had. I don't know what it was about. But I know we were in Norfolk at the time, living in a converted byre. And she was kneeling in front of the grate, trying to kindle some wet timber; and I can't remember what I said but I remembered her reply; and what she said was: 'If you leave me, Frank, I'll kill myself.' And it wasn't that she was demented – in fact she was almost calm, and smiling. But whatever way she looked straight at me, without fully facing me, I recognised then for the first time that there was more of her mother than her father in her; and I realised that I would have to be with her until the very end.

He walks upstage. Pause.

I must have walked that floor for a couple of hours. And all the time the landlord never moved from behind the bar. He hadn't spoken since the wedding guests left. He wouldn't even look at me. I think he hated me. I know he did. I asked him for a last drink. Then he spoke in a rush: 'Get to hell out of here before they come back, mister! I know them fellas – savage bloody men. And there's nothing you can do for McGarvey – nothing nobody can do for McGarvey. You know that. 'I know that,' I said. 'But if you do nothing for him, mister, they'll kill you. I know them. They'll kill you.' 'I know that, too,' I said. But he rushed into a back room.

I poured a drink for myself. A small Irish with an equal amount of water. The thought occurred to me to get drunk but I dismissed it as . . . inappropriate. Then I heard the car return and stop outside. A silence. Then Donal's head round the door.

'McGarvey's here. But he's shy about coming in. Come you out. They're waiting for you out there in the yard.'

'Coming,' I said.

He puts on the hat and overcoat and buttons it slowly. When that is done he goes on.

There were two yards in fact. The first one I went into – it was immediately behind the lounge – it was a tiny area, partially covered, dark, cluttered with barrels and boxes of empties and smelling of stale beer and toilets. I knew that wasn't it.

Then I found a wooden door. I passed through that and there was the other, the large yard. And I knew it at once.

I would like to describe that yard to you.

It was a September morning, just after dawn. The sky was orange and everything glowed with a soft radiance – as if each detail of the scene had its own self-awareness and was satisfied with itself.

The yard was a perfect square enclosed by the back of the building and three high walls. And the wall facing me as I walked out was breached by an arched entrance.

Almost in the centre of the square but a little to my left was a tractor and a trailer. In the back of the trailer were four implements: there was an axe and there was a crowbar and there was a mallet and there was a hayfork. They were resting against the side of the trailer.

In the corners facing me and within the walls were two mature birch trees and the wind was sufficient to move them.

The ground was cobbled but pleasant to walk on because the cobbles were smooth with use.

And I walked across that yard, over those worn cobbles, towards the arched entrance, because framed in it, you would think posed symmetrically, were the four wedding guests; and in front of them, in his wheelchair, McGarvey.

The four looked . . . diminished in that dawn light; their faces whiter; their carnations chaste against the black suits. Ned was on the left of the line, Donal on the right, and the other two, whose names I never knew, between them.

And McGarvey. Of course, McGarvey. More shrunken than I had thought. And younger. His hands folded patiently on his knees; his feet turned in, his head slightly to the side. A figure of infinite patience, of profound resignation, you would imagine. Not a hint of savagery. And Ned's left hand protectively on his shoulder.

And although I knew that nothing was going to happen, nothing at all, I walked across the yard towards them. And as I walked I became possessed of a strange and trembling intimation: that the whole corporeal world – the cobbles, the trees, the sky, those four malign implements – somehow they had shed their physical reality and had become mere imaginings, and that in all existence there was only myself and the wedding guests. And that intimation in turn gave way to a stronger sense: that even we had ceased to be physical and existed only in spirit, only in the need we had for each other.

He takes off his hat as if he were entering a church and holds it at his chest. He is both awed and elated. As he speaks the remaining lines he moves very slowly down stage.

And as I moved across that yard towards them and offered myself to them, then for the first time I had a simple and genuine sense of home-coming. Then for the first time there was no atrophying terror; and the maddening questions were silent.

At long last I was renouncing chance.

Pause for about four seconds. Then quick black.